Hello Brains!

An mBIT science based guide to listening within

By Amy Mercer and Laura Masters

To request permissions, contact the publisher at
freedomhousepublishingco@gmail.com or amy@abundanceenterprise.com

Paperback: 978-1-952566-58-5
Hardback: 978-1-952566-59-2
Ebook: 978-1-952566-62-2

Printed in the USA.
Freedom House Publishing Co
Middleton, ID 83644
www.freedomhousepublishingco.com

Did you know you have more than one brain?

Science says so!!

Come along with us to meet your three brains!

Each brain has a special job to do for you that helps keep you happy, safe, and healthy.

And, if you get very quiet and breathe,
you will learn how to listen.

You can listen to the deep knowing of each and help them all work together.

Working together they combine compassion, creativity and courage with action and become your very special, unique brand of wisdom.

The world needs the wisdom and magic of you!!!

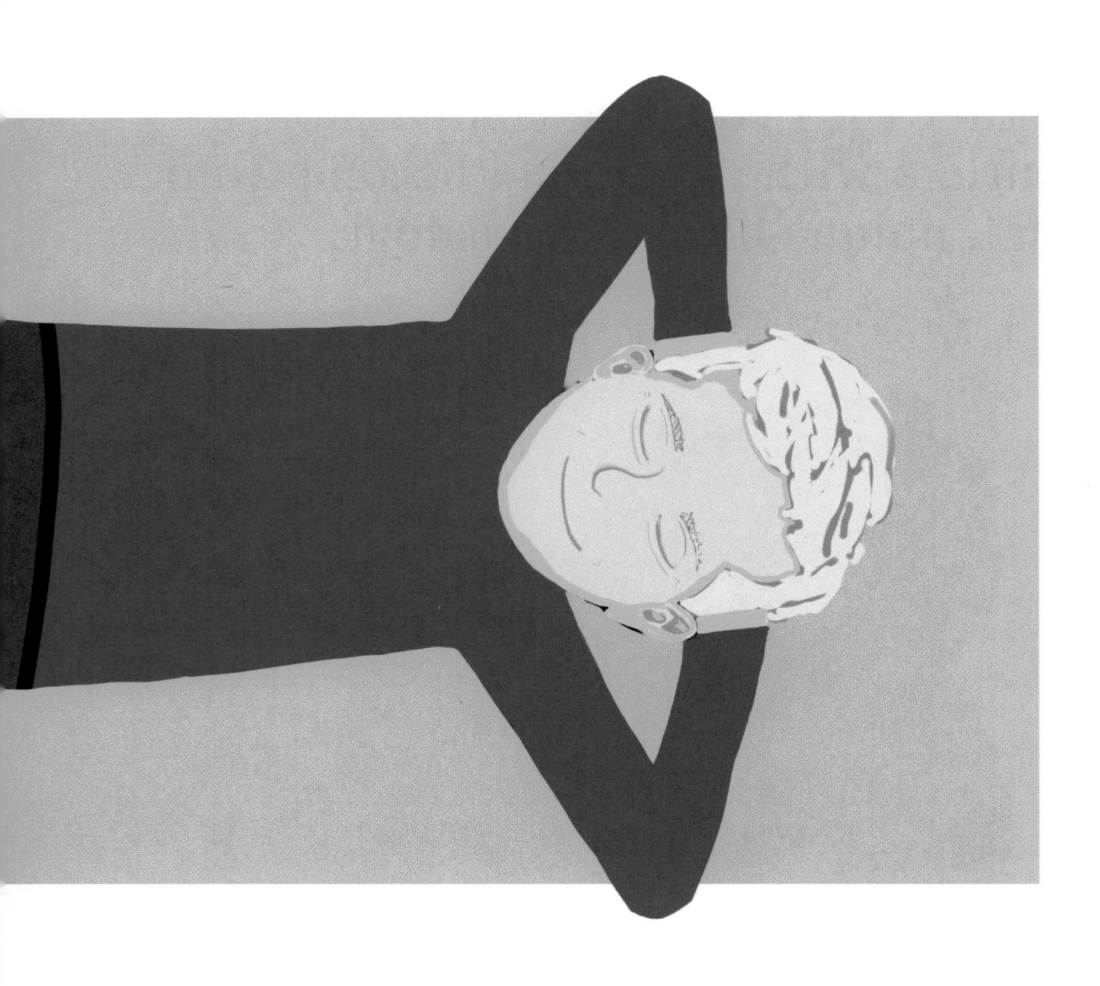

Breathe

deep down into your body,
six seconds in,
six seconds out.
Feel your loving heart and imagine
a friend, a pet, a memory,
someone or something you deeply love...

Connect to your heart...

Put your hands near your heart as you listen...

Your heart brain speaks in pictures, feelings, colors and simple words. It is the leader when feelings, desires, values and connections are to be understood. It can be the soft voice of your joy, love, peace, inspiration, and perhaps loneliness. Your heart speaks louder when strong feelings arise: passion, anger, pain and justice.

When you are balanced, your truest dreams emerge with compassion.

Hello Heart!

Breathe

deep down into your body,
six seconds in,
six seconds out.
Feel your loving heart and imagine
a friend, a pet, a memory,
someone or something you deeply love...

Connect to your mind...

Put your hands on your head as you listen...

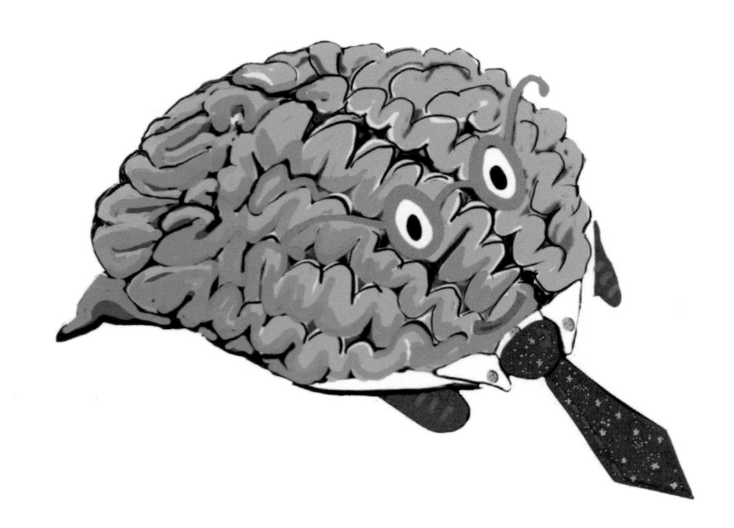

Your head brain speaks in words, (lots of words), complex words, pictures, stories and big ideas. It is useful when sensing the world around you and determining what things mean and why. It loves to interpret, understand, plan and create. It can be super bossy and loud and sometimes thinks it's in charge of everything. But when it is a bit quieter and more generous, it is the clever, funny, intricate architect of your life. The head brain can build or break down walls, accomplish goals and dreams, and inspire magical adventures.

When you are balanced, you design your life with creativity.

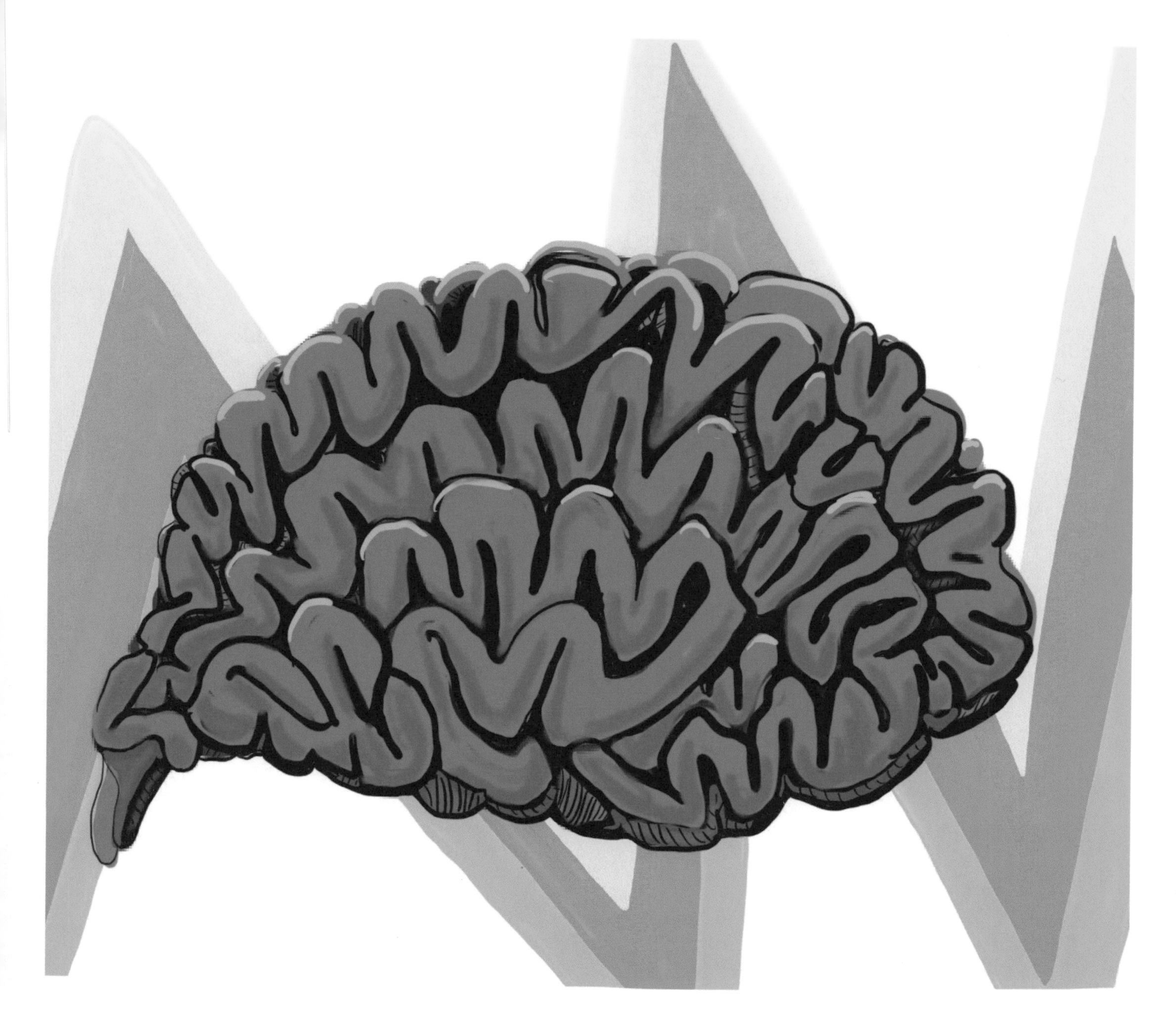

Hello Head!

Breathe

deep down into your body,
six seconds in,
six seconds out.
Feel your loving heart and imagine
a friend, a pet, a memory,
someone or something you deeply love...

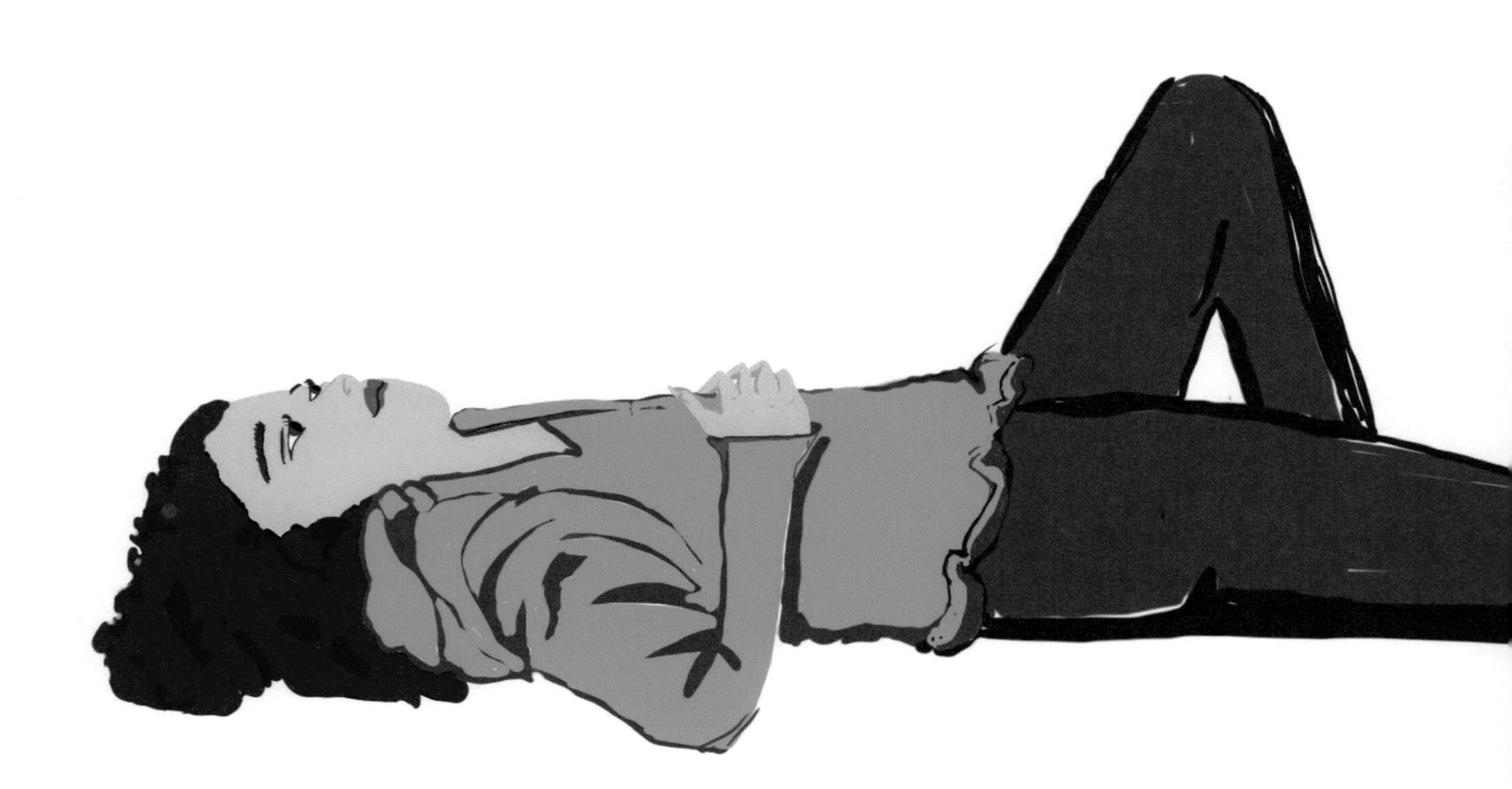

Connect to your gut...

Put your hands on your tummy as you listen...

Your gut brain is the strong silent type; very primitive. It speaks in dreams, intuitions, very simple words, feelings and sounds (burp, toot, grumble...). So give your gut some time! This brain is all about You!

Its purpose is to keep YOU safe and give YOU energy and motivation to express YOURself. It guides you towards what is good and pure and healthy and informs you what to avoid or dump. This is the "home safe home" of your deepest and most authentic you.

When you are balanced, you are courageously you.

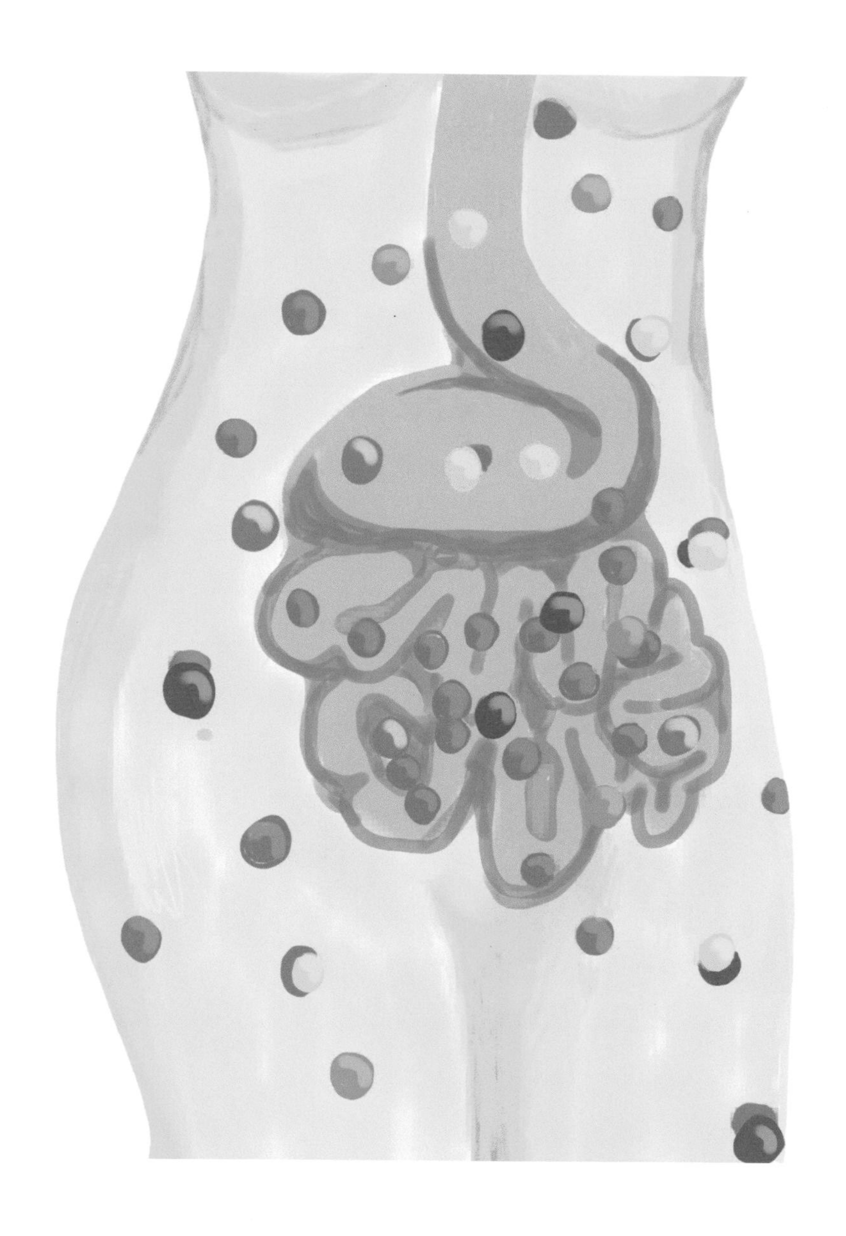

Hello Gut!

When we listen with honor to each brain,
its inspiration and ideas,
its complaints and fears...
When we use the smartest of each in all that we do,
when brains work together with respect and cooperation,
this is when we are at our very best

and the
Magic of ME
appears!

Hello Wisdom!

The End

Your Authors: Amy and Laura

Amy and Laura have been friends for over 25 years. Both have raised children and are certified life coaches, educators and presenters. They study extensively in the fields of psychology, neuroscience, education, and learning with an intent to understand the ways in which our brains learn, rewire and facilitate personal growth and happiness. After becoming certified trainers of mBIT, Amy and Laura wanted to bring mBIT to as many people as they could as it provides a method to connect with and act from our authentic selves with compassion, courage and creativity. They continue to look for ways to provide tools to individuals, families and businesses that make life more meaningful, abundant and fun.

*This book is based in neuroscience and on behavioral research. The technique for communicating with our three brains are presented by Grant Soosalu and Marvin Oka in their book mBraining.

Find out more by going to **Abundanceenterprise.com** and **mBraining.com.**

AbundanceEnterprise.com

Thank you so much for purchasing and reading this book! We are passionate about making an impact in the world by bringing more awareness to our multiple brains and the neuroscience-based approach mBIT (multiple brain integration techniques) that can help people live more fulfilling lives.

CHECK OUT OUR FREE GIFT

As a free gift we'd like to offer you our Balanced Breathing Guide. A tool anyone can use to bring themselves quickly back into a state of calm coherence!

Testimonial on Balanced Breathing

"After learning this balanced breathing technique I used it with my six year old while was having a meltdown. I calmly told him as soon as we breathe for 3 minutes we can go back to playing. I put a timer on my phone and by the time we were done he was calm. He even asked me 'why did breathing make me feel better?' I will use this technique from now on!"

– Jessica Tietjen, mBIT coach & mother to a six-year-old boy and twin 2-year-old girls

Learn a little more about us...

Who are we and what do we do?

Abundance Enterprise uses the principles of mBIT and the process of mBraining to offer a way to reteach these lost/forgotten skills (which are the birthright of every human being) to people who are yearning to reconnect with their own deep wisdom. mBraining equips individuals to live life authentically and freely as who they truly are and want to be every moment, every day. We coach individuals using mBIT and are also certified to train mBIT coaches.

What is mBIT (multiple brain integration techniques)?

mBIT is a suite of tools grounded in neuroscience and ancient wisdom traditions. Beginning with a balanced nervous system, mBIT tools effectively align the three neural centers and their natural strengths in the appropriate sequence, to find true, deep wisdom. mBraining is the process of embracing and applying those learned tools to make decisions and take action in the world as one's authentic self. mBraining is also the name of the book and website used by Grant Soosalu and Marvin Oka to represent, introduce, and teach about mBIT.

Made in United States
Troutdale, OR
09/23/2023